Nature's Embrace

the poetry of Ivan Bunin

translated from Russian by Patrick Wang

Copyright © 2020 Patrick Wang. All rights reserved.
First Edition
ISBN: 978-1-7356865-1-6

Ivan Alekseyevich Bunin was born in 1870 in Voronezh, Russia. He published his first poem in 1887 and his first short story in 1891.

In 1903 he won the Pushkin Prize for his collection of poems *Foliage* and his translation of Longfellow's poem *The Song of Hiawatha*. He was awarded a second Pushkin Prize in 1909 for his collection *Poems 1903–1906* and translations of poems by Byron and Longfellow.

In 1920 he emigrated with his wife to France where he would spend the rest of his life. In 1933 he was the first Russian to be awarded the Nobel Prize in Literature.

He died in 1953 and is buried at the Russian Cemetery in Sainte-Geneviève-des-Bois outside Paris.

* * *

Widen, chest, and burst open for welcoming
Springtime feelings—you transient guests!
Nature, such an embrace you are offering,
Merging into your sumptuousness!

You, the heaven, the faraway eminence
Blue expanse so interminable!
You, the verdant vast countryside limitless!
You are why I am craving a soul!

1886

THE POET

The poet, sorrowful and spartan,
A pauper, poverty controlled,
In vain the chains of destitution
You strive to shatter with your soul!

In vain you wish for your defiance
To overcome your wretched luck
And, prone to sparkling devotions,
You wish for confidence and love!

Forever poverty will poison
Bright moments reveries appear,
And making you forget the vision
And bringing you to bitter tears.

And then, exhausted by misfortune,
Forgetting fruitless, cruel times,
From hunger you will die,— and blossoms
Your burial cross will intertwine.

1886

* * *

The fields are darkening, becoming sea-like, boundless,
In doleful glow of sunset drowning, fading on—
And gentle night floats through the steppe's expanses
     Once silent sun is gone.

Just gophers in the rye conversing with their whistling,
Or the jerboas, so mysterious, like ghosts,
Who float along in rapid, soundless, leaping
     To vanish into smoke...

1887

OCTOBER SUNRISE

Night turning paler, the crescent is setting
    Sickle of red on the creek.
Silvery meadows with somnolent misting,
All the black reeds turning dampened and smoking,
    Breezes are rustling the reeds.

Peaceful in town. In the chapel a lantern
    Darkening, burned for so long.
Quivering gloominess chilling the garden
Filling with billowing cold from the steppeland...
    Gradually ripens the dawn.

1887

* * *

On my own I leave the home at midnight,
Clinking, frozen footsteps on the ground,
Stars are strewn in garden's darkened crown,
And on roofs—straw whitened by the moonlight:
Where the mourning midnight will lie down.

November 1888

* * *

Soul beneath the body yearning,
    Blubbering and sings,
Triumphing and then resenting,
    Calling out in grief.

O the good and gracious! Waken
    Have mercy on the people!
Meager, worthless, wretched humans
    In goodness and in evil!

O when Christ in crucifixion
    Heavy head he hung!
There are saints in heart commotions,—
    Give to them a tongue!

1889

MOTHERLAND

How they hurl ridicule towards thee,
How they, o motherland, laugh up
How you are simply ordinary,
Your shabby looking patchy hut.

That son, so nonchalantly cocky,
His mother an embarrassment—
So weary, shyly, sorrowfully
Among his city dwelling friends.

He smiles and looks so piteously
At she, who traipsed from far away
To visit him, and for this journey,
Her every penny she had saved.

1891

THE NIGHTINGALES

First flourishing and then decaying,
Beyond the manor thunder crashed,
Along the lane the poplars braying,
Along the glass the twilight dashed.
And all below the clouds are pouring;
And all more tangible, more new
Tempestuous blowing winds entangling
The weeping skies and field perfumes.
The fields of grain bent to the edges...
And from the gardens, from the vales—
From everywhere the wind projected
The eager strains of nightingales.

But over maples over poplars
The wintery whirlwind flew by...
The moistureless grass murmured sighs,
The window slamming with a clatter,
The lightning flashes fire...
And then at home above the shelter
I heard the crash of sudden thunder
And then a crushing roar... All over
At once it thoroughly died down,
The darkened garden quiet now,—
Come bountifully, sweepingly
Resounding showers of the spring.

Upon the edge a bent depression
Of grain... And from the garden sails
Again that sonorous projection
The eager strains of nightingales.

And as it weakened languorously,
The rain dissolved and thunder died.
Then overwhelmed the lane completely
The sweetly scented warmth of night.
Steam, motionless and aromatic,
Stood with the grain. Earth slumbering.
Beneath the clouds a dawn just lucid
A strip of scarlet firing.
From gardens, also from the darkness
Where flowers blossomed in the vales,
Poured out throughout resounding thickets
The brightening song of nightingales.

1892

SPRING

Snow is melting—sun is brightly
Blazing over fields at noontime;
In the glare the humid breezes
Through the forest-fields are roaming.
But the fields are still deserted,
But the forests still are speechless;
Only pine trees, just like harp strings,
All are humming uniformly.
Underneath their muddy humming,
In the secret pinewood thicket,
Sweetly sleeps the springtime-princess
In sarcophagus of snowflakes.
Sleeps,— and shortly in the valleys
Sun will thaw the whitened snowfall,
Streams will go off percolating
Through the valleys and the gullies.
Forest birds will start their swarming,
Rooks will grumble and be joining—
All will blossom turning verdant,
Forest grove reanimated.
And returns the April-princess
From that far off foreign country
At the dawn, when in the valley
Bluish fog is dissipating,

At the dawn, when from the sunshine
Comes the scent of forest needles,
Comes the scent of earth reheated
And the April flowers blooming,
Sun is beaming and he's bowing
Down above the speechless princess
Nestling to her princess lips and
With his steady heated kisses,
She is shuddering and frightened,
Opens up her lengthy lashes,
Peeps, emblazes—and now beaming
Brightens all the world with loving.

1893

* * *

...And I had a dream, it was fall I suppose
And one chilly night I was coming back home.
Alone I was walking down shadowy roads
To farmsteads familiar, to my home town...
And cracked all the branches of willow that froze
From turbulent winds on the elderly boughs...
The village was sleeping... With dread, like a thief,
I entered the courtyard deserted and bleak.

And I clenched my heart where the pain amplified,
When I had a look all around in the light!
The roof it was hovering, corners collapsed,
The flooring was creaking each step on my path
And smelling like ovens... Forgotten, decayed,
Forever forgotten, our dear childhood home!
And why was I here? What remains to be shown,
And if it remains—well then what does it say?

And I had a dream, I was walking all night
Through gardens, where winds pirouetted and whined,
I searched for the spruce that was planted by dad,
I searched for the rooms, where the family convened,
Where mama had once rocked my crib with her hand
And tenderly, sadly had fawned over me,—
With lunatic anguish I try to call out,
And uncovered gardens they whistled and howled...

1893

TRINITY

Inviting all to pray, the church bells now are sounding,
Through sunny blazes over all the fields it rings;
The distant flooding arcs in azure now are drowning,
The river in the meadow burning, glittering.

And in the village church there is a mass this hour:
Green grass is strewn to cover all the podium,
The altar, radiant, has been adorned with flowers,
The amber luster of the candles and the sun.

And loudly sings the chorus, joyfully, discordant,
And through the windows breezes bring in fragrances…
Your day is now, my brother, weary and obedient,
Your spring festivities, so calm and luminescent!

You have this day from your considerable sowing
Brought to this place your gifts of simple offerings:
The garland woven from the branches of young birch trees,
Hushed sigh of sorrow, prayer—and humility.

1893

CYPRESSES

Deserted Yaila mountain sitting smoking eddies,
With misty skies departed from the distant sea,
A noisy surf below, the harbor waves are boiling,
And here—a heavy sleep and everlasting grief.

Then let the living cities, bordering blue harbors,
Ring out and radiate with life... The broods this way
The cypresses they will await—in silent rigor
Death will ascend this place to plunder fatal gains.

Life does not bother them, perfunctory and daily...
No just the evening tolling coming from the banks
With echoes resonating, ringing, and bemoaning,
With whitened crosses keeping vigil over graves.

1896

* * *

Foliage in the garden drops...
In this old familiar garden,
Early morning I'll depart
For wherever I may wander.
Foliage spinning, rustling,
Wind comes flying in with bluster,
Buzzing garden, flustering,
Somberly it then will wither.
In my heart—it's merrier!
I will love, I'm younger, younger:
Why regard this walkway whirr
Or the autumn chilled and somber?
Wind will drag me far and wide,
Ringing out my song will scatter,
Ardent heart awaiting life,
     Seeking rapture!

Foliage in the garden drops,
Couple spinning after couple...
Lonely I'm delirious
Through the foliage I shuffle,
In my heart—there is fresh love,
And I wish to hear an answer
To my heart song—let it come
Let me meet that carefree rapture.

Why then is my soul so sore?
Who will grieve, will give me pity?
Wind then stirs a dusty roar
All along the walkway birch trees,
Driving back my weeping heart,
In the somber garden spinning,
Yellow foliage departs
    With sad wailing!

1898

* * *

Dreams again, so sweetly captivating,
Same intoxicating dream of joy,—
Darling eyes are slyly tantalizing,
Fawning smiling lures me to rejoin.

Still I know,— I'll be deceived again as
Vanishes this dream first flash of day,
But until unhappy day commences,
Smile at me some more—deceive away!

1898

* * *

At midnight I walked in on her,
As she was sleeping,— moon reflected
Into her window,— and the blankets
Were dangling, glowing satin swirls.

Upon her back she lay asleep,
In nakedness her breast divided,—
And calm, like water in a chalice,
Her life was standing in a dream.

1898

* * *

Someone sings tonight, he's tireless.
Roaming far into the fields of darkness,
Voice rings out with plaintive recklessness,
Singing of his bygone bliss and wishes.

Opening up the window, sitting by.
You were sleeping… Long I listened keenly…
From the field that smelled of rain and rye,
Came the night so redolent and chilly.

That within my soul the voice awoke,
I don't know… My soul now fills with sorrow,
And with tenderness I loved you so,
Just as once before you loved me also.

1899

HEAT

Sunbaked sand so fervently is sparkling,
Arid heat on sink stones of the seine.
Out at sea—dead calm and tender splashing
Of the crystal waters on the sand.

Seagull in the brilliant air is glistening…
Down her shadow comes right over me—
And in solar radiance is drowning…
Blinding heat is bending me to sleep.

I lie down, from heat intoxication.
Dreams of gardens and a breezy cove,
All the cypress trees in fixed formation
Guard the water canon baritone.

Antique marble under yew tree branches
Winding over them is younger rose,
And the blazing harbor between cypress,
Positively like blue fire flows…

1900

FOLIAGE

The woods, just like an ornate home,
That's golden, crimson, also purple,
A merry wall of polychrome
Stands over incandescent meadow.
The yellow stands of birches mold
The azure blue resplendent glow.
Like towers, all the fir trees looming,
Among the many maples bluing
And here and there, through foliage: holes
For glimpsing sky, like little windows.
The woods now smell of pine and oak,
That for a summer season sizzled,
And autumn widow in repose
Is entering her motley home.

Today in a deserted meadow,
Within a yard that is immense,
The airborne spiderwebbing tendrils
Resplendent, just like silver nets.
And all day long it has been playing
Inside the yard, the final moth
And, like a small white petal dropped,
And on the spiderwebbing staying,
Just basking in the warming sun.
Today so bright an ambience,
With such a deathly hushed quintessence

In woods and in blue altitudes,
Perhaps in quiet interludes
You'll hear the leaves and their rustling hiss.
The woods, just like an ornate home,
That's golden, crimson, also purple,
Stands over sunshine brightened meadows,
By silent sorcery transformed;
A blackbird cackles, quickly flying
Among the underbrush, of glowing
Cascades of amber foliage;
And playing in the sky will lunge
A flock of dissipating starlings—
Then once again the stillness comes.

Yes happiness' final flickers!
Already autumn knows that these
Profound and wordless days of peace—
Are omens for prolonged foul weather.
The woods' deep silence chills the bones
And from the onset, at the gloaming
Magenta fired gleam and golden
Infernal blaze lit up the home.
Then everything goes dark and somber.
The moon ascends, the woods withdrew
As shadows fell upon the dew
And everything turned cold and whiter
Within the glade, within the site
Of lifeless autumn thicket nighttime,
The autumn is a lonely fright
Abandoned on a silent night.

But then there is another silence:
Prick up your ears—it will expand,
Delivering a frightening whiteness,
As creepingly the moon will stand.
Then every single shadow shortens,
Transparent hazes standing by
And then like witnessing a vision
Of misty heaven's lofty heights.
O, deathly dreams of midnight autumn!
O, frightful miracles of night!
The damp and silver mists encircle
The bright unpopulated meadow;
Woods, brimming with the whitest light,
Its comeliness solidified
Like prophesizing its own dying;
A night owl who is mute: just sits
Yes, blankly from the branch he'll glimpse,
Then suddenly will burst out laughing,
Falls from the heights with blustering,
His silky wings are softly flapping
Then sits again on shrubbery
And through his bulbous peepers staring,
That high-eared head of his he bops
From side to side, with pure amazement;
The woods are standing in enchantment,
So full of light and pallid fog
And dampening, the foliage rots…

Do not expect: that in the morning
The sun breaks through. With rain and fog,
Cold hazes can be suffocating,—
No wonder night has traveled on!
But Autumn will preserve profoundly
All things that she has suffered through
That speechless night, when solitary
She shut herself within her room:
How pines enrage beneath the spume,
How bleak and desolate the night
And in the meadow wolfish eyes
Fluoresce their fiery green bloom!
The woods, a home with no attendant,
The whole thing tarnishes and fades,
September spinning through pine thickets,
Dismantling roofs along the way
And flings damp foliage at the entry,
That's where tonight first snow is falling
To melt, to then kill everything.

In distant fields the horns are blaring,
Their brassy ringing modulates,
Like bitter cries, they're propagating
The misty, miserable glade.
Through blustering trees, beyond the valley,
In wooded depths they dissipate,
The gloomy goat horns spew their howling,
They call together dogs of prey,
And their resounding voices rage,
The blustering desert tempest swelling.

The rain comes down as cold as ice,
The foliage spins throughout the meadow,
As lengthy caravans of geese go
Above the woods in huddled flight.
But days go by. Already smoke fumes
Arise like pillars with the sun,
The woods are crimson, without motion,
A silver frosted ambiance.
And wearing her white fur shugai,
Her pallid face now freshly cleansed,
To see the woods for one last meeting,
Emerges Autumn on her steps.
A cold, bare yard. And at the entrance
Among two aspen all dried out
Blue valleys noticeable now
And the expansive desert marshes,
That lengthy road that's leading southward:
Where far from winter storms and blizzards,
And far from winter blasts and cold
The birds had flown to long ago;
And so for Autumn in the morning
That's where her lonely path will lead,
Forever from the woods of pine trees
Her disembosomed home she'll leave.

Let go, you woods! Let go, goodbye,
The days they shall be gentle, pleasant,
And soon they'll fade these newly frozen
Decaying silver-coated sights.
How strange it'll be to leave that whitened

Deserted day and all the cold
And all the pines, and home abandoned,
And rooftops of the village fold,
And sky, and all without a border
To walk away and leave the field!
I'm sure the sables will be thrilled,
Along with all the ermines, otters,
They'll bask, cavort, and run around
On banks of snow drifts on the ground!
And then, some wildly dancing shaman,
Upon the naked taiga whirls about
And pulls in winds from tundra, ocean,
Carousing snowfall spins around
And like a savage beast is growling.
Your ancient home they'll be destroying
They'll only leave the stakes and then
Upon that empty skeleton
They'll hang up icicles all over,
And there will be against blue sky
An icy palace that will shimmer
With silver, and with crystal lights.
At night, among the streaks of white,
On heaven's vault ascend the lights,
The stars of Pleiades vivacious—
That hour, within the hush of night
When frosty phosphorescence blazes,
The hey day of the Northern Lights.

1900

* * *

I'm grateful, Lord, for every thing of yours!
Who following a day of stress and sadness,
Bestows of me the evening sunset cure,
With neverending fields and with blue mildness.

Today I am alone—invariably.
But then the sunset spilled exquisite gusto,
It melts the Evening Star entirely,
And quivers all throughout, just like a gemstone.

My somber fate I've happily assumed,
And there is comfort in sweet recognition,
That I'm alone in silent contemplation,
That I'm estranged from them and speak—with You.

1901

* * *

Upon the highest peak, on snowy mountain,
I carved a sonnet with a steely blade.
The days roll by. Perhaps up to the present
The snows maintain my solitary trace.

Upon the highest peak, so blue the heaven,
Where winter light will blithely radiate,
With just a glimpse of sun, I drew my blade,
And on the emerald ice floe wrote my poem.

I am amused to think, some poet may
Decipher me. Uneasy in the lowlands,
With pleasing greetings he can't tolerate!

Upon the highest peak, so blue the heaven,
Upon midday, a sonnet I engraved
For only those, who live upon the mountain.

1901

* * *

Stars, I will forever sing your praises!
You remain mysterious and youthful.
Since my childhood days I've humbly witnessed
Runes within the dark abyss that twinkle.

As a child I loved you without thinking,—
Like a fairytale your friendly winking.
As a youngster it was with you only
I confided secret hopes and suffering.

Looking back on early declarations,
Searching out in you a gracious pattern...
Days will pass—and you'll forever glisten
On my grave, my grave long since forgotten.

And, perhaps, someday I'll understand you,
And the dream, perhaps, will see fruition,
Earthly hopes and suffering then destined
To be merged with mystery of heaven.

1901

* * *

To the distant north the sunset had retreated,
But its scarlet solar traces keep all night.
In the dark and quiet fields, sweet clover scented,
Over earth a feeble sheen of demi-light.

These—the nights of trembling adolescent dreaming,
Pre-dawn duskiness in tender semi-sleep.
These—the nights of mournfulness and reminiscing,
Sunset meditations on the bygone spring.

1901

*   *   *

That peaceful gaze, the way a doe will gaze,
And all that I had loved in it so dearly,
I still had not forgotten in my grieving,
But nowadays your image is a haze.

And there will come a day—when grief will lessen,
When all the reminiscing fades to blue,
Where there is neither happiness nor gloom,
And there will only be forgiving distance.

1901

THE STREAM

A stream among the arid sands…
Where is he hurrying and fleeing?
And why between these meager lands
Does he so staunchly pave his journey?

The sky is pale from all the heat,
No cloud within the azure ferment,
It feels like all the world now meets
In rounds of sand in vivid wastelands.

And he, transparent, talkative,
As if he knows, that eastern sojourns
Will lead to seas, where bays will sit
Before him and explode horizons—

And cheerful flow accepted through,
Beneath expansive bounteous heaven,
Into the vastitude of blue,
Into the sacramental bosom.

1901

* * *

When all along the rolling boat, the foam is creeping
And sky between the rigs turns blue upon its peaks,
I love your pallid face, unfortunate Selene,
Your melancholy gaze, accompanying me.
I love the fishing tunes beneath the rippling cadence,
And freshness of the waters—nightly, waves will groan,
And founded on a vision, the alluring maiden,
And my haphazard course, my solitary boat.

1902

DEATH

Beneath the moon a calmly quiet graveyard...
The arms of crosses, lilacs, also stones...
But on our tomb—beneath the marble rampart,
A stretched out shadow, like a darkened ghost.

It scares me. Seeing my sepulchral double
In moonlight, like it's waiting for some thing...
I go—and like a feeble slave, the shadow
Again will crawl, again obeying me!

1902

FORGOTTEN FOUNTAIN

The amber palace it went scattering,—
Along the drafty passage leading homeward.
September's chilly breath is gathering
And barreling throughout the empty garden.

It covers up the fountain all with leaves,
It lifts them up, by bearing down abruptly,
And then, just like a frightened flock of starlings,
Throughout the dried out glade they're circling.

From time to time a girl came to the fountain,
Her shawl dragged over foliage as she went,
And long she gazed at it without disruption.

Her face—is hardened disillusionment,
Entire days she roams just like a phantom,
And days roll on... There's no one they lament.

1902

FROST

So vividly ablaze the stars,
The Milky Way so clearly shimmers,
That entering a snowy yard
It all will phosphoresce and glimmer.

The light is falling silver-blue
From the Orion constellation,
Like fantasy, it spills on you
On frosty snow descending heaven.

And snowy smoke of phosphor stirs,
And you can see it gently flicker
Upon your icy scented fur
Tossed airily upon the shoulders.

Those dangling earrings glistening,
And pupils growing even darker
They stare with greedy ecstasy
Through eyelashes of sprinkled silver.

1903

AFTER THE BATTLE

Spear pierced, he shed his helmet, fell to rest.
The mound was rough and hollowed out. The fevered
Noon burned his back, the chain mail jabbed his chest...
The withered heat of autumn huffing northward.

He died. Then ossified and petrified,
His heavy head upon the ground collapses.
And breezes toss his hair from side to side.
Like feather grass, like lifeless sedges.

And all the ants began to swarm inside...
But apathetic silence all around now,
And far along the naked countryside
A spear, that penetrated in mound, stuck out.

1903

* * *

Stars blazing all over earth now deserted,
Holiest Canis formation majestically shines:
Suddenly everything's dark—and a fiery serpent
Over the shadowy earth slashes red through the sky.

Traveller, don't be afraid! Desert marvels are plenty.
This is no eddy, but rather the jinn in pursuit,
This is the archangel, servicing God full of mercy,
Aiming at night demons hurtling his golden harpoon.

1903

EVE OF KUPALA

In the shady grove fog doesn't whiten,
Through the shady grove walks Virgin Mary,
Through the greenery of hills, through valleys
Gathering by night God's herbal plantings.

Their remaining lifetimes end this evening,
So it is, and sunlight's almost over:
In the west it's blocked by black spruce needles,
Gold iconostasis of the sunset...

Quickly in damp valleys, fall the shadows,
Quickly in blue meadows, fall the dewdrops,
Underneath the dew it smells of lungwort,
Through the grove there shines a golden halo.

Just like fog, Her clothes are alabaster,
Azure eyes exactly like the starlight.
She will gather various herbs and flowers
And then carry them before God's altar.

Night comes—only night for them remaining,
And tomorrow scythes will cut them lower,
No, not cut—sun ruins them with ardor.
To the Son declares the Virgin Mary:

"Look, beloved Son, will you regard
How the earth had blossomed, how it flourished!
Yes the age of earthly joys is fleeting:
In the world is Death, who rules the Living."

Christ replies: "But Mother! It's not sunlight
Covering the earth, it is night's darkness:
Death won't ruin seeds, it's only cutting
Just the flowers from the earthly seeding.

And the earthly seeds will not diminish.
Death will mow—and Love will sow moreover.
So rejoice, Beloved! You'll continue
Take this comfort through the age of passing!"

1903

* * *

Awakened suddenly, without a reason.
I dreamt of something sad—and instantly
Awakened. Through bare branches of the aspens
I gazed upon the misty lunar ring.

The manor in the autumn keeps her quiet.
The house all draped in dead of midnight calm.
And then, just like a child abandoned, cried out
The big-eared little owlet in the barn.

1903

THE POET'S GRAVE

At his marmoreal tomb—sorrowful thronging of cypress:
Heaven's blue bosom shines happier through all the trees,
Angel created above him with lamp of life toppling over:
Brighter the fires will blaze, prostrating low in the grave.

1903

LONELINESS

The wind, and the rain, and the fog
  In a frigid, deserted, wet place.
Here life until spring will be gone,
  Until spring all the garden's a waste.
I'm alone at the dacha. No light
At my easel, from wind no respite.

Just yesterday you were with me,
  Though to me you had looked drained of life.
The evening drizzling scene
  How you seemed to me just like a wife...
Well, goodbye! Until springtime arrives
I'll survive on my own—with no wife...

Today it goes on without end
  The same clouds—mountainside, mountainside.
Your trace under rain by the step
  Becomes blurred, from the water inside.
And it hurts me to watch it alone
In the gray afternoon as it drones.

I wanted to shout as you dashed:
  "Turn around, how I feel like we've merged!"
But for womenfolk there is no past:
  Out of love—you're a stranger to her.
Well! Some chimney fire, some alcohol...
And you know, maybe I'll get a dog.

1903

IN THE MOUNTAINS

The golden disk is tumbling
The moon in gaps of darkened storm clouds,
And melts in them, and through the steam
On stony cliffs its luster streams out.

But there on the horizon see:
The moon is standing, steam is hovering...
Eternity keeps Time from running,
And all our lives are waxen dreams!

1903-1904

JASMINE

The blooming jasmine. Verdant thicket
This morning to Terek I'll go.
Among far mountains—brilliant, basic
Explicit clear-cut silver cones.

The river bellows, sparks and shimmers,
The fervent woods with jasmine notes.
Above—the summer and the winter:
Blue sky and January snow.

The woods die out, subdued by frizzle;
But jasmine blooms luxuriant.
In vivid azure and ambrosial—
The mountaintop's magnificence.

1904

EVERLASTING LAMP

She's quiet, she is now collected.
But joy will not return: that day
When they had showered on his casket
Damp earth, joy turned its back on her.

She's quiet,— her soul has now
Been emptied, a sepulchral chapel,
Where day and night above the tomb
An everlasting lamp is burning.

1903-1905

GHOSTS

No, those departed did not die for us!
    According to an ancient Scottish legend,
Invisible to us their presences
    Will come at midnight for a visitation,

And dusty harps, just hanging on the wall,
    When touched by them infuse with magic
And sleeping strings awaken to recall
    The most lamentable, ambrosial music.

We call the ancient legends fairytales,
    We're deaf by day, day's not for understanding;
But in the twilight, fairytales prevail
    And in the silence trustingly we're listening.

We don't believe in ghosts; but still for us
    Who suffer loving, suffer parting's anguish...
I've listened to them, heard them more than once,
    That most lamentable, ambrosial music!

1903-1905

THE BLACK STONE OF KAABA

It formerly had been a precious jasper,
Its luminance was indescribable—
Like consecrated Jannah gardens' color,
Like days of sun and spring on mountain snow.

First Gabriel for Abraham's assistance
Discovered it among the sands and reefs,
Then wisemen kept it at the temple entrance,
And there the pearly mass sat sparkling.

But ages passed—from all throughout the cosmos
The prayers came hastening to it, and streams
Flowed to the temple, far away and hallowed,
From hearts, of overburdened anguishing...

Allah! Allah! Your precious gift does not glow—
Now dimmed from tears of human suffering.

1903-1905

* * *

Along the road, a luscious green spruce forest,
With recesses of fluffy snowy hoards.
Within it walked a stag, robust, thin-legged,
He pitches back his thorny, heavy horns.

He leaves his traces. Here's a trampled footpath,
And here the tree was bent where white teeth gripped—
And numerous coniferous crosses, remnants
Of scattered crowns upon the snowy drifts.

Again the trace, deliberate, in patches,
And then—a leap! A distant field to plunge
To leave behind the beastly rut—and branches,
The chipped and worn out horns out on the run.

How very easily he quit the valley!
How wildly, freshly overrun with strength,
Impetuously, mercilessly merry,
From death he carries beauty far away.

1905

MYSTICISM

In chilly chamber, moon illuminated,
    I entered then a child.
The dappled shade on framework antiquated,
    The shiny, waxy ground.

Like at the altar, here there were high windows,
    And there—the orb of night,
And whitest snow, and through the powdered billows—
    The hundred year old pine.

In terror, at the doorway I stopped moving:
    Just like the altar air,
Throughout the chamber incensed gloom was smoking,
    Across the silverware.

But eyes land on the sky: the sky's behaving,
    The moon is bright and crisp—
And terror left... How often, all for nothing
    The young are scared of mist.

Now it's been ages since the mystic temple
    And silly shadowed swirls:
When you go over the abyss—be careful
    To gaze at azure worlds.

1905

DOUBLE RAINBOW

A double rainbow—and the gold, exotic
Precipitating spring. The west is set
To flash its beams. Upon the highest branches
Of orchards, lush from May-time elements,
Against a somber cloudy luminescence
A spot of blackened bird. It's all revived
By rainbow light so violet and verdant
And by the honeyed scent of rye.

1903-1906

NURSERY

From fir and spruce the room is darkening,
Inanimate and ancient. Still predating
Whatever you may see. And evening
Will blush across the sunset's frosty gilding.

The lighted pattern, soft and borderless,
Upon the reddened walls will rest its shadow—
And all this dreary, dreary winter dusk
On the estate, in this abandoned alcove!

And from the corner window you will gaze
And think how life unfolded previously...
Well after all you're sitting in the place
That used to be our nursery!

1903-1906

HEAD OF STONE

The grasses dried from heat and are all dead.
The steppe—unbound, but blue there in the distance.
Here's bone remaining from the horse's head.
Here's more—a Head of Stone before us.

What listless views of flattened tissue!
What savage understanding of the body!
But I'm somehow still afraid of you... who
Is smiling at me diffidently.

O spawn of ancient wickedness!
Were you not formerly the thunderbearer?
—No god, no god imagined us. It's us...
Our slavish hearts are God's creator.

1903-1906

THE BIRD

We tied a bird to everyone's neck.
—Koran

On all of you—on every purple mantle,
Upon the dusty sackcloth of each slave—
There is an amulet, a bird-like symbol,
There is a secret sign, that sign is—Fate.

And from antiquity, from His beginning,
He came, among the caskets, purposeful:
He, passing by, His traces indicating
The inauspicious whitened brightened skulls.

Upon them khamsin blows a heated hazing,
The sand is rushing at their bone remains.
An owl, a stranger, will remain this evening
Among the pit of graves.

1903-1906

LAPWINGS

The lapwings had started to cry, keen and vivid
        The azurite clear springtime light,
And wrapping the road, where there's sun—where it's torrid,
        Is wormwood that's graying and dried.

In gray colored fields—and on baby blue lakefronts,
        On farmland—the purplish ground.
The lapwings are crying—from light in the open,
        From joy—they will cry and will clown.

1906

SNAKE

As long as March hums in the woods with naked
Enmeshing branches,— flat and featureless,
I sleep within the knothole. Sleep in solid foliage,
Chilled sleep—I wait: the spring is imminent.

Already in the clouds, like sapphire windows,
Transparent azure... Dried up at the root,
And butterfly in steamy beams of sun glow
Drops to the foliage... Under it I move,

I am evolving rings, intoxicating
In warming rays... I sluggishly unreel—
Once more I blossom, burn away, I'm changing.
I'm decked out now in copper, turquoise, steel.

Where woods are drier, full of motley foliage
And yellow flies, there's motley braid—the snake.
The hotter is the day, more flies more golden—
More poison I will make.

1906

WALTZ

Petals eventually cooling
Baring the lips, emerging dewy,—
Chamber of sailing, sailing lengthy
Melodies happily yearning.

When chandeliers and mirrors dance
A crystalline mirage emerges—
And blowing, blowing ballroom breezes
Of aromatic warmth from fans.

1906

MUHAMMAD IN EXILE

Spirits hurtled over all the wasteland
Over petrified ravines at gloaming
Melancholy words of his resounded
Like a wellspring God had been neglecting.

Barefoot on the sand, he bared his bosom,
Sitting there he uttered lamentations:
"To the wasteland and to desolation
I've stayed true, removed from all my loved ones!"

And the Spirits spoke: "How unbecoming
For the feeble Prophet it's all over."
And the Prophet with regret, now calming
Answered: "I complained about the boulders."

1906

MOSCOW

Here in the Arbat's olden alleyways,
A truly special place... in March, in spring.
With abject freezing in the mezzanine,
Too many rats, but come the night—just lovely.
By day the drops are falling, warming sunshine,
By nighttime frosting over, turning spotless,
And bright—and seeming very Moscow-like,
Old-fashioned, at a distance. I sit down,
Not lighting up a lamp, beside the window,
The moonlight pouring in, I look toward
The garden, to infrequent stars... How tender
The nighttime sky of spring! How comforting
The springtime moon! Now melting down, like candles
The crosses on the ancient church. Through branches
In deepest sky affectionately glisten,
Like golden plated hammered helmets,
The heads of tiny copulas...

1906

BY CANDLELIGHT

Aquamarine underpinning,
Golden arrowheaded spear...
I recall a winter evening,
From my early childhood years.

With my hand I shield the candle,
See, again, I have inside
Living, ruby-colored blood flow
Gently glowing in the light.

Aquamarine underpinning
Golden arrowheaded spear...
Childhood's all my heart is keeping:
Nothing else is mine, I fear.

August 1906

HOPELESSNESS

In northern country there is rosy moss,
And there are dunes so silvery and silky...
But all the dark resounding pine tree tops
Will sing and sing above the sea, like heartstrings.

Now hear them close. Lean on, become the tree:
Through fearsome noise can you hear delicacy?
But they are also—singing half-asleep...
Up north some hopelessness is reassuring.

1906-1907

THE LAW

In the name of God, eternal mercy!
He, who gave the reed for holy words,
Quoth: observe the written word devoutly
Do exactly as the tongue assured.

Take this law, and take along its fetters.
Either spurn—or honor your whole spirit:
Do not be the donkey toting records
Just because they have been told to bear it.

1906-1907

MANDRAKE

Flower of the Mandrake blossoms over grave landscapes,
Over underground coffins buried next to black gallows.
The decaying dead juices will then nourish the Mandrake—
And the blossom emerges like a weed that is feral.

Brother Cain, who cultivated Mandrake from poison!
God with merciful judgement may then spare the assassin.
But the hangman is different: it's from Hell you have risen,
Flower, laden with poison, you, God hasn't forgotten!

1906-1907

ODIN

He was glancing out west—as the sunlight was vanishing.
      Angry flames shining over the sea.
He was cold on the cliff—his old cloak it was fluttering
      From the wintery winds that won't ease.

Leaning onto his blade, he looks out at the crimsonly
      Colored scales of the limitless swells.
But he doesn't see waves—he is only imagining
      Sullen thoughts as his countenance tells.

Ancient world. He is too. Odin's cloak an apology,
      Rust of centuries—on iron blade...
Blackest raven Huginn, sorry offspring of Memory,
      On his shoulder will stay.

1906-1907

SATURN

Disseminated conflagrative kernels
On never-ending planets take root fast.
And at the sight of stars I'm quickly humbled:
The Maker's fathomless and ageless craft.

But then at midnight in the east ascending:
The corpse of Saturn—and like lead it flickers...
So absolutely sinister and rending
This business of yours, Maker!

1906-1907

QUAGMIRE

      The swamps in peaceful northern provinces
Come autumn dusk they're stranger than the cemetery.
      Blooms blooming. No idea what size they're really
Because they have their secret subsoil, sleepy depths.

      At times, there's something sad we must remember...
But what? That we from earth and God are far away...
      And embers will be born in quagmire graves...
In darkness will be born the light... We—swampy embers.

1906-1907

RESURRECTION

One torrid April noon, along the gravel
That runs between the efflorescent gardens
A monk went by, a very tall Franciscan,
Towards the southern seaside monastery.
"Who's there?" the porter asked behind the entry.
"A Christian brother," answered the Franciscan.
"And who is it you're seeking?" "Brother Gabriel."
"He's occupied right now—he writes on Sundays."
The monk then snatched a rose from off the fencing,
And hurled it in the yard—looking unhappy
He left. And then the rose behind the fencing
On marble splashes into blackest ashes.

1907

WINE

—Up on Yaila beech trees turning leafy,
And the slender pines are reddening:
Why then in the northland, separately,
Can the soul perceive, that it is spring?

"On the days, when grapes live with the vine leaf
Wildly blossoming, their destiny
Is in cellars, where it's dark and chilly,
Gold fermenting wine eventually."

1906-1908

LUCIFER

The doves flew into holiest Sophia,
Nefarious mullah. The Erechtheion was mute.
The gods of Homer's epic poems withdrew
To freeze and bore themselves in bare museums.

The mighty Sphinx, delivering on sadness,
Lay in the sand. Israeli alien
Is gathering the weeping, rusty tablets.
And Christ departed greedy Bethlehem.

Here's Eden, Lebanon. The dawn burns crimson.
The snowy peaks—like silk. On slopes the herds
Flow through the caves. In meadows—sea haze hidden…

Pure days of childhood faith! It's Abel's earth!
Behind the bare Jabal Al-Sharqi mountains
Is shimmering, declining, Lucifer.

1908

STAR WORSHIPPERS

The world will not forget the ancient faiths.
Star worshippers of desert cities,
The pallid heat of planets—on your face,
You honor stones like sanctuaries.

Your province now in ashes torched by flame,
Your God had specified such fearsome tablets,
That for eternity his name—
You will not even dare to speak it.

Muhammad, Christ, they pass like dreams.
And to this day you will remember
Devotion to the planet mysteries
And to that nameless ancient Power.

1906-1909

DOG

Dream on, dream on. It's all so cramped and bleak
When you are focusing your golden peepers
On blizzards in the yard, on snowy flitters,
On rumbling, smoking, broomstick poplar trees.

You sigh, and then you're curling up to warm
My feet—and now you're wondering... We have been
Here languishing—we want our scene transformed,
Another desert... past the Permic mountains.

You will recall things alien to me:
The hoary sky, the tundra, ice and teepees
All in that freezing, savage way you see.

And I will always share with you my thinking:
I am a man: like God, I am obliged
To yearn for all the countries all the time.

1909

EVENING

O happiness forever recollected,
And happiness is all around. There's more
Here in this autumn garden past the woodshed
And pours though windows in the air so pure.

At endless heaven's lightest, brightest limits
A cloud arises, shines. Since long ago
I've tracked it... We have seen and known a pittance
And happiness will go to those who know.

The window's open. Birdie's squeaking, perching
Upon the windowsill. And wearily
I turn from books just momentarily.

The evening's falling, and the sky has emptied.
And from the barn I hear the harvesting...
I see, I hear, I'm happy. All in me.

1909

MIDNIGHT

November midnight, damp. A village sleeps,
Beneath the moon, all chalkiness, all paleness,
All overwhelmed by an unanswered silence.
The sound of tides in their triumphant sweep.

The captain's flag is getting watery.
On top, above the mast, above all objects
The muddy mists, escaping to the east,
The moon it glides as on a mirrored whiteness.

I head to cliffs. The sound's more menacing.
The glow's a mystery, more dim and saddened.
The waves are pounding posts beneath the cabin.

Far off—a gray abyss. There is no sea.
And boulders, washed in hissing grayish lather,
Are glistening below, like seals in slumber.

1909

NIGHT CICADAS

The coastal gravel and the naked sea cliffs
The walls of plains in lunar luminance.
With crystal ringing sky to crop field fuses.

The flowers, grasses, wheat are full of them,
Though never silent, still they won't awaken
The apathetic pre-dawn somnolence.

Night spreads it shadow, shores will chill and dampen,
Night drags its golden net—it's exiting,
And soon the glittering will wane and weaken.

But sings the steppe. As wheat is ripening,
The soul is filling. Earth is calling: hasten
To love, create, intoxicate in dreams!

From ashy stars, extending from the zenith,
To earth, to cooling dreams in lunar light,
The filament of trembling crystal courses.

This ringing woven from a swarm of lives.

1910

WITHOUT A NAME

The mound dug up. Sarcophagus tremendous.
He sleeps, guard-like. An iron blade he holds.
Above him sing the picture-scripted sagas,
Without a sound, the idiom intoned.

But with his visor low—his face is hidden.
But on his rusted armor lies a cloak decayed.
A warrior, chief. But Death his name has stolen
And on his blackened steed he sped away.

1906-1911

THE BIRCH

Up on a distant ridge, on borderland
Of empty sky, there is a whitened birch tree:
The trunk, contorted by the storms, and flatly
Extended dried out branches. Here I stand
Admiring it, in yellow, barren acres.

It's dead. Where there is shade, there's salty layers
Of resting frost. And with the sun so weak
It will not warm. And not a single leaf
Appears upon these branches, brown and reddish,
The trunk stark white against green emptiness.

But autumn—world of saddened dreaminess,
A world reflecting on the past, on losses.
Up on a distant ridge, upon the edge
Of empty fields, a birch will stand alone.
But easily. Its spring was long ago.

1906-1911

THE STEWARD

The night lamp burns within a frigid, dreary
Enormous chamber meagerly and dark.
The house beset by wicked rumbling, rustling
As hundred year old limes on windows knock.

The rain pours down all night. It seems that someone
Is coming to the porch... Then far away
A scream is carrying... And then there's problems:
The leaky rooftop through the ceiling drains.

Again wake up, again adjust the basins!
With just this meager lamp by which to grope,
With sleepy eyes so desperately swollen,
In only underpants and shabby coat!

1906-1911

SUNDIAL

Those watches with enamel, that when dark
Can easily maintain their hasty movements,
They long ago went silent. And in gardens
The nettles grow all over hills of rot.

That radiating pendulum, emboldened
To regulate its span within a box,
In dusty attic archives it lies dormant.
And crypts will keep the nameless ashes locked.

But we have labored righteously and sacred.
At midnight stars will make us silvery,
By day the sun engoldens—until sunset.

Our copper dial piece turned completely green.
But now the arrow on our dial's roundlet
Leads God himself. With all in harmony.

1906-1911

* * *

Ocean underneath the vivid moon,
Warmer, loftier and pale complected,
Slower surges, propagated smooth,
Summer lightning ardently ignited.

Piles of clouds climb up the mountain grade:
For the holy Forces, Gabriel censes,
Incense at the dark of royal gates
How the fire-breathing censer flashes.

Indian Ocean
1911

SAADI'S PRECEPT

Be generous, like a palm. And if you may not be, then be
Like trunks of cypress trees, be straight and simple—honorable.

1913

GRANDPA

Grandpa eats a pear upon the stove-bench,
Gums bite into fruit that's ripe and sweet.
Lifting up his shoulders' bony remnants,
Pulls them to his skull, just like a freak.

Eyes—like currants, with a beastly savage
Emptiness and sadness. All forgot.
He's already stocked with coffin canvas,
But for food—still some ferocious spark.

Smells: from everywhere he gathered,
Looking at the stove-bench, at the bunk
Waiting for excruciating Power...
Hurriedly and hurriedly he'll—munch.

1913

THE WORD

The speechless coffins, bones and mummies,—
    The word's just for the living:
From ancient dark, in cosmic cemeteries,
    Where just Inscriptions ring.

For us there is no other patrimony!
    And you must learn to keep
Them best, in days of suffering and fury,
    Our timeless blessing—speech.

Moscow
1915

THE POET

A deeply dug well has cold water within,
The colder it is, then the purer it is.
The shepherd who's careless will drink from a puddle
And water from puddles he gives to his flock,
But good ones seek wells where a bucket they'll drop,
With rope to the rappelling carefully coupled.

A valuable jewel, was dropped in the night,
A slave seeks it out by his cheap candle's light,
His sharp eyes are searching the dusty road travelled,
Within his dry palm there's a ladle he grips,
To shield from the flame all the darkness and winds,—
And know: he'll return with the jewel to the castle.

1915

THE BRIDE

As I was plaiting girlish braids,
Upon the ledge beside the window,
Night constellations in bouquets,
Beside the sea that gently rustled,
And then the steppe shook half awake
With its mysterious remarking...
Now who before you came my way?
Yes who that night before the wedding,
My soul exhausted by the strain
Of loving, fondness and affliction?
To whom I yielded unrestrained
Before the latest separation?

1915

* * *

At the darkened Nubian shanties
Where we gave the horses water.
Toasty evening, easy, shady
Bit of Nile saffron glimmer.

At the darkened Nubian shanties
Someone sang, so cooling pining:
"I am homesick, I am grieving
All because I am good-looking…"

Mice were fluttering and trembling,
Oxen in the slurries slumber,
Shanties smelling bitter, smoky,
Bit of Nile stellar glimmer.

1915

* * *

Pyramids amidst the fevered golden sunset,
On the river Nile, charming all the tourists,
With the sailboats gleaming silkily in water
Alabaster Luxor ship makes its escape.
At this hour, of vivid palm trees on the river,
When the glass in Cairo shines with scarlet polish,
Carriages convey khedives, while guides retreated
From their overlords to lounge at the cafes.

And the river Nile offered lilac southward,
To untamed Nubia, to the swelling Rapids
And the world remaining alien, a stranger,
As with Khufu, with Cambyses… I will bring
Longbows from there and the copper-greenish quiver,
Shield of hippo leather, javelin elastic,
Chain mail from Sudan and also fur of cougar,
What I'll do with these—I'm wondering.

1915

AT THE END

The false Messiah walked the earth,—
I wasn't tempted, I could see,
Their liturgy was lust and slur
And speech—like cymbals rattling.

These self-interested prophets,
Liars with impoverished reason!
Star, still in the eastern province
Still amongst the dark profusion.

At the end your time elapses:
Again old earth is cursed—again
Satan drinks from brimming chalice
The idol's bloody sacrament!

1916

YOUTH

In withered forest cracks a lengthy whip,
In shrubbery the cattle set to blather,
And blooming snowdrops falling in blue drips,
And underneath the oak tree leaves will whisper.

And rainy clouds go promenading by,
And into grayish fields fresh winds come blowing,
And heart concealing pleasurable longing,
To live, as steppe is, empty and sublime.

1916

* * *

Sun of the midnight, the shadows are purplish
Falling in yellowed out hollows of waves.
Sun does not warm—upon visages serious
Crashes the light of the icy cold rays.

Gone Solovetsky monastery's last crucifix.
Nothing—from here to the pole. On the sea
Leisurely mists for the runaway diocese—
Three fellow elders and all in bare feet.

1916

THE HORSE OF PALLAS ATHENA

The high priests were singing, the gates swinging open—adoring
    People fell down on their knees:
A towering horse, with his head painted golden, is soaring
    Into the sun's brilliant beams.

Woe to you, Ilion! Populous, glorious, colossal,
    Woe to you, Ilion, woe!
Due to the roaring of priests and wild cries of the people
    Prophesies screamed by Cassandra were lost to the droves!

1916

THE LAST BUMBLEBEE

Darkly velvety bumblebee, aureate shoulders,
Inconsolably droning melodious themes,
Tell me why would you fly into humanly shelter
As if somehow you're grieving with me?

Out the window, the light and the vividness sizzle,
Final days of sereneness and blistering heat.
Do some soaring, some schmoozing—seek out a dry thistle,
On your red colored pillow, go sleep.

You were never intended to know human anguish,
That for years the fields haven't done well,
That a miserable wind before long will abolish
A dry aureate bumblebee shell!

1916

POMPEII

Pompeii! How many times now have I walked
These alleys! But Pompeii you are so solemn
To me as lifeless as a graveyard plot,
More dead and cleaner than a new museum.

I am to blame, all things I have forgot:
Where so and so had lived, which fairy had been
In naked walls, no rooftops, rafters lost,
Gone circle dancing, waving drapes transparent!

I can recall trace Roman evidence,
The rubbings from their wheels outside the gateway,
The gardens, valley mist, Vesuvius.

It was the spring. Like honey in a safe place,
My greedy heart had joyfully saved up
My surplus strength—and only life I loved.

1916

THE OLD APPLE TREE

All in snow, and fleecy, smelling sweetly,
All of you is ringing blithesome buzzing
Of the bees and wasps, from golden sun.
Getting old, compassionate companion?
Never fear! For I have never seen such
Vigorous old age on anyone!

1916

* * *

And ages passed, and Eden's walls had fallen,
And then its Garden went to seed, went wild,
And by the night the beasts they were not frightened
By scintillating Sword up in the sky,
And Man he then re-entered Eden—vainly
He wished to see his golden dream begone—
And Satan, triumphing malevolently,
In Eden's place erected—Babylon.

June 29, 1916

LIGHT

We've been bestowed not emptiness, not dark:
Light's everywhere, it's faceless and forever...

At midnight. Gloom. Basilica's hushed specter,
But take a harder look: it's not all dark,
From the abyss, a blackened vault ascending,
There on that wall, a narrow window parts,
Just visible, far in the distance, bleary,
The shimmering enigma of the shrine
From night to night throughout eleven centuries...
And all around you? Can't you sense beyond these
Slick crosses on the stony floor inside,—
The caskets of the saints, below in slumber,
The terrifying silence of such spots,
Abounding with unmentionable wonders,
Where from behind the altar the black cross
Is raising up its difficult embracement,
Where all the mysteries of Crucifixion
The father-god invisibly protects?

There is such light, that darkness can't afflict.

July 7, 1916

* * *

The icon, blackened plaque discovered
In earth, — when virgin soil was plowed...
Who lit a candle here before her,
Their grievances and love avowed?
Who consecrated her presenting
The prayer of a beggar, slave
And with his staff and her then coming
Out to the steppe, to rustling grain—
And, worshiping the sultry whirlwinds,
Stribog's descendants, lifted then
Above the dusty, fussy field land
Her shield of heavenly command?

In a dream
July 21, 1916

* * *

The coastal shores are pale and faint,
    Illuminated by the moon.
The lowly moon, the garish waves,
    Their crests in goldenness festooned.

And in the distance gleaming waves
    Are hammered out like armor scales.
On sand a sailor sits dismayed
    And next to him a lady pales.

Their final moments side by side!—
    And all the dunes are radiant.
He is the groom and she the bride,
    Whenever will they meet again?

He's staring at the midnight moon
    And tediously wondering:
"And yet again upon these dunes,—
    The kisses then the severing?"

Indeed: the marching centuries,
    The generations rotating—
The sailor sits! Eyes hungering,
    Delighting and admiring...

Life flashes by just like a dream.
        And now the morning glimmers
The whisky playing tricks with me
        And distance makes it vaguer.

Delight and pain my soul assault
        Forever I'll remember how:
The bitter tears of heat and salt
        Confounded fervor in my mouth!

July 22, 1916

* * *

No, Mister, really there's no Wheel in life:
No Wheel: there is a rim, the spokes, and bushings,
There is a road, a steed, a need for driving,
There is a rumbling, thud and iron tire shine.
And all the world, and us? Don't we resemble
The Wheel? Yes, it resembles you I feel.

And there's the fact that Wheels all cost more rubles:
Now there's a Thought on Wheels.

July 25, 1916

* * *

Night and crimson colored lightning.
      Here again:
Spark—against the darkened shrouding
      Smooth, immense.

Constantly on stones and ridges,
      Plummeting
Flash of crimson lights up heaven
      Instantly,

It lights up, and it is blinding,
      On the sea
Coastal waves of water boiling
      Milkily.

It lights up, succinct, unsteady,
      Our beguiled
Fretful faces as our ladies
      Try to smile.

And against this easy, wayward
      Little romp
Rolls demonic rumbling over
      Mountaintops.

1916

LILY OF THE VALLEY

Through bare groves a coldness tumbles...
You lit up amongst the burnt,
Deadened foliage... I was youthful,
I composed my earliest verse—

And forever linked with spotless
Spirit of my youthfulness
Dewy-freshened aqueousness
Of your piquant redolence.

1917

EPITAPH

On this earth you resembled a marvelous bird come from heaven
Touching down on the branches of cypress, among gilded graves.
Like a flute in noon thickets, the ring of your youthful expression,
And from darkest eyelashes the radiant suns emanate.

Therefore fate noticed you. Saw the earth is no place for this presence.
It is only in Eden that beauty can know no restraints.

1917

UNFADING LIGHT

There, in fields, within graveyards,
    In old groves of birch trees,
Without tombs, without bone shards—
    Just the realm of blithe dreams.
Summer breezes are shaking
    Lengthy flourishing boughs—
And I feel it approaching
    Light that comes from your smile.
Tombstone, crucifix fading—
    Until now all I face
Schoolgirl uniform only
    And a radiant gaze.
Are you now solitary?
    Aren't you with me again
In our previous story,
    I was different then?
On terrestrial circle,
    Now in my current day,
All my classical, youthful
    Self has long gone away!

1917

* * *

This ephemeral life of endless variation
How I shall relentlessly amuse myself,
This: the early sun, the smoky habitations,
Park with scarlet foliage falling in slow motion,
And familiar, faded bench, there's you as well.

For the future poets, whom I'm never meeting,
God leaves secretly—the memory of me:
I become their dreams, becoming disembodied,
Inaccessible to death,— superbly ghostly
In this park so scarlet, in this silent peace.

1917

* * *

And the flowers, and bees, and the grasses, and durum,
And the azure, and afternoon heat...
Then the Lord one day asks of the prodigal children:
"With your life upon earth were you pleased?"

I forget everything, I could only remember
Roving fields between grasses and wheat—
Through sweet tears knowing I couldn't possibly answer,
I collapse at his merciful Knee.

1918

* * *

Ancient cloister up against the moonlight,
On the wooded hillock, over river waterways,
On the walls are chalky pale-blue highlights,
Marble of the heavens, white, with sapphire bluish trace.

And upon this heaven, here within these clouds,
Heavenly abyss within a concentrating pall,—
Temples within tiny bulges wearing golden shrouds,
Charms of paradise are just beyond the gleaming wall.

1918

* * *

—Give me, grandma, potions for bewitching,
Love like in the ballads, easygoing,
      Soothing to behold.

—Sweetest child, I can't do what you're asking:
For these potions do not grow in groves,
      But in graves are waiting.

1918

* * *

The bird it has its nest, the beast it has its hole,
    How grievous was my youthful heart that instant,
When I set out departing from my father's home,
    Apologies hearth of my childhood!

The beast it has its hole, the bird it has its nest,
    How beats my heart, its loud and grievous impact,
When I walk in, and cross myself, a renting guest
    With my already worn-out knapsack!

1922

RUSSIA

O, unwept tears so poisonous!
O, futile flame of disapproval!
He's blessed who shatters on the gravel
Your, Harlot, newborn little ones,
Born into this untamed occasion
Your pleasures—our tormented blows.

He's blessed who strikes you with a bow
God's consecrated vindication!

1922

YEAR 1885

It was the spring, and life it was so easy.
Fresh grave is gaping open to hereafter,
But life was easy, like a cloud that's fleeting,
Just like the smoke, that flutters from the censer.

The earth was blossoming like new soil does,
So blissfully, it all was laid before me—
The first of verses and the first of love
Together with the grave and spring they found me.

And that was you, a simple prairie bud,
Forgotten by me, faded and elusive,
And in my morning days death conquered me, like God,
And led me to a timeless world exquisite!

1922

THE ROOSTER ON THE CHURCH CROSS

And sailing, flowing, with the crow,
So high above the earth afloat!
The firmament regathering,
And he up front—and all will sing.

The song about, how we must live,
That we will pass, that daily slips
The years, the flowing centuries—
As if a cloud, as if a stream.

The song about, how all's deceit,
How fortune lands for just a blink
And father's home, and fellow mate,
And set of kids, and kids they make,

How only death will never dim,
And yes, God's church, his cross, and him.

1922

* * *

The lofty blooms not native to these sites
Grew up on graves in grass formations,
And all the overflowing lights of heaven
Were watching them from elevated heights.

And marvelous was Venus, like the moon,
Our faces, hands in pale illumination—
And sea in her sepulchral shroud protection
Was gloom, completely motionless and gloom.

NIGHT STROLL

Moon watches over the forested meadows
Passes across remnants of the cathedral.
In the dead abbey two skeletons jaundiced
Wandered around in the moonlit quiescence.
Lady and knight, who's inclined to the lady
(Skull that is noseless and skull that is eyeless):
"This brings us closer, for isn't that crazy
Each of us happened to die from Black Pestis.
I am Tenth Century,— if you'll forgive me
From curiosity which did you come from?"
And she is answering as she is grinning:
"Oh, well how young you are! I'm from the Sixth one."

1938

* * *

You were living in silence and peace.
Beside old-fashioned yellowing walls,
Under white colored ceilings of chalk,
With a window that looked to the east.

Bit of sun on a wintery morning,
And your spirit is already soaring:
On the floor the light's dazzling glow,
In the corner a toasty hot stove.

All the books in the case, all in order
On the desk notebooks wait for the writer,
There's a sweet smelling flower bouquet...
You think, "Happiness really is lame!"

October 18, 1938

* * *

I was alone in midnight's kingdom,—
Until the dawn I could not sleep.
As noisier, triumphant, broadened
Vibrations came from distant seas.

I was alone in all the cosmos,
Just like its god—and just for me,
For me alone primordial echoes
Abysmal voice of booming peace.

November 6, 1938

NEL MEZZO DEL CAMIN DI NOSTRA VITA

The April days just outside Naples,
When it's so damp and wintery,
The heart so sweet with God's own peace...
The valley orchards pinkly dappled,
And in them cyan mists convened,
The darkened colony in silence,
The grey extended willow branches,
Asleep inhaling jimson weed
From land that's plowed and fertilizing...
The sullen lurking dangers rising
In runes of thickened smoky palls,
How clouds discharging on the mountains
Upon their steepened slopes would bluen...
These days, I always will recall!

1947

* * *

Night and rain, and in the house a lone
Window in the dampened darkness shone,
Chilly house stands quiet and decayed,
Like a crypt among the muted graves,
Crypt, where long ago dissolved the dead,
Great-grandfathers, grandfathers, and dads,
Where a single blinded night lamp keeps
And upon the bench the geezer sleeps,
Long beyond his masters he has stayed,
Friend, eyewitness to our bygone days.

WREATHS

There was a feast thrown in my honor, on my pate
A laurel wreath, an emerald crowning:
It quickly chilled my brow, as icy as a snake,
In hall of feting, scorching, crowding.

There'll be a new wreath—based on all the gossiping
It will be made of darkened myrtle:
In hall of graves, of everlasting shade and sleep,
Its chill upon my brow will be eternal.

1950

NIGHT

Icy night, a mistral blows
(Still it's not died down).
Shine through windows and remote
Mountain, naked mounds.
Golden stationary light
Off to bed it's gone.
No one in the world tonight,
Only me and God.
Only He perceives of these
Stone cold griefs of mine,
I from everyone recede…
Coldness, mistral, shine.

1952

INDEX

Widen, chest, and burst open for welcoming.................. 1

THE POET.. 2

The fields are darkening, becoming sea-like, boundless..... 3

OCTOBER SUNRISE.. 4

On my own I leave the home at midnight.................... 5

Soul beneath the body yearning............................ 6

MOTHERLAND.. 7

THE NIGHTINGALES...................................... 8

SPRING.. 10

...And I had a dream, it was fall I suppose................ 12

TRINITY.. 13

CYPRESSES.. 14

Foliage in the garden drops.............................. 15

Dreams again, so sweetly captivating..................... 17

At midnight I walked in on her........................... 18

Someone sings tonight, he's tireless...................... 19

HEAT.. 20

FOLIAGE.. 21

I'm grateful, Lord, for every thing of yours............... 27

Upon the highest peak, on snowy mountain.................... 28

Stars, I will forever sing your praises........................... 29

To the distant north the sunset had retreated.................. 30

That peaceful gaze, the way a doe will gaze..................... 31

THE STREAM.. 32

When all along the rolling boat, the foam is creeping......... 33

DEATH... 34

FORGOTTEN FOUNTAIN.. 35

FROST... 36

AFTER THE BATTLE.. 37

Stars blazing all over earth now deserted........................ 38

EVE OF KUPALA... 39

Awakened suddenly, without a reason............................ 41

THE POET'S GRAVE... 42

LONELINESS... 43

IN THE MOUNTAINS.. 44

JASMINE.. 45

EVERLASTING LAMP... 46

GHOSTS... 47

THE BLACK STONE OF KAABA...................................... 48

Along the road, a luscious green spruce forest................. 49

MYSTICISM	50
DOUBLE RAINBOW	51
NURSERY	52
HEAD OF STONE	53
THE BIRD	54
LAPWINGS	55
SNAKE	56
WALTZ	57
MUHAMMAD IN EXILE	58
MOSCOW	59
BY CANDLELIGHT	60
HOPELESSNESS	61
THE LAW	62
MANDRAKE	63
ODIN	64
SATURN	65
QUAGMIRE	66
RESURRECTION	67
WINE	68
LUCIFER	69
STAR WORSHIPPERS	70

DOG	71
EVENING	72
MIDNIGHT	73
NIGHT CICADAS	74
WITHOUT A NAME	75
THE BIRCH	76
THE STEWARD	77
SUNDIAL	78
Ocean underneath the vivid moon	79
SAADI'S PRECEPT	80
GRANDPA	81
THE WORD	82
THE POET	83
THE BRIDE	84
At the darkened Nubian shanties	85
Pyramids amidst the fevered golden sunset	86
AT THE END	87
YOUTH	88
Sun of the midnight, the shadows are purplish	89
THE HORSE OF PALLAS ATHENA	90
THE LAST BUMBLEBEE	91

POMPEII..92

THE OLD APPLE TREE.. 93

And ages passed, and Eden's walls had fallen................... 94

LIGHT...95

The icon, blackened plaque discovered...........................96

The coastal shores are pale and faint............................. 97

No, Mister, really there's no Wheel in life........................99

Night and crimson colored lightning.............................100

LILY OF THE VALLEY... 101

EPITAPH...102

UNFADING LIGHT... 103

This ephemeral life of endless variation......................... 104

And the flowers, and bees, and the grasses, and durum...... 105

Ancient cloister up against the moonlight....................... 106

—Give me, grandma, potions for bewitching...................107

The bird it has its nest, the beast it has its hole................ 108

RUSSIA... 109

YEAR 1885... 110

THE ROOSTER ON THE CHURCH CROSS................ 111

The lofty blooms not native to these sites....................... 112

NIGHT STROLL..113

You were living in silence and peace................................ 114
I was alone in midnight's kingdom.................................. 115
NEL MEZZO DEL CAMIN DI NOSTRA VITA............ 116
Night and rain, and in the house a lone........................... 117
WREATHS...118
NIGHT.. 119

www.ingramcontent.com/pod-product-compliance
Lightning Source LLC
Chambersburg PA
CBHW072203100526
44589CB00015B/2340